To:

....

From:

....

Date:

....

GUIDED JOURNAL

100 DAYS
to brave

Unlock Your Most
Courageous Self

ANNIE F. DOWNS

ZONDERVAN®

ZONDERVAN

100 Days to Brave Guided Journal

© 2020 by Annie F. Downs

Requests for information should be addressed to:
Zondervan, *3900 Sparks Dr. SE, Grand Rapids, Michigan 49546*

ISBN 978-0-310-45522-6

The author is represented by Alive Literary Agency, 7680 Goddard Street, Suite 200, Colorado Springs, Colorado 80920, www.aliveliterary.com.

Art direction: Patti Evans
Interior design: Kristy L. Edwards

Printed in India

20 21 22 23 24   REP   10 9 8 7 6 5 4 3 2 1

I have not yet reached my goal, and I am not perfect. But Christ has taken hold of me. So I keep on running and struggling to take hold of the prize. . . . We must keep going in the direction that we are now headed.

—Philippians 3:12, 16 CEV

Introduction

*D*ear friend,

This says a lot to me, you being here. It says you are feeling what I sometimes feel—like there is more than this. Your "this" may look different from my "this," but it's true all the same.

So I'm really glad you're here. And I hope you'll stick around all the way to the end because there is something here for you. At the least, it's an invitation to run after a life that might require a bit more courage but will certainly offer more joy and more than "this." At the most, everything changes. And that can be pretty awesome.

I hope you will take this journal with you for the daily story you are writing about your life. These one hundred days are special to me, and I hope they will be to you as well. I've pulled together some of my favorite thoughts on courage and bravery and mixed them with lots of new ones that God and life and people have taught me over the last few years. And I think that together with whatever God is already doing in your life, this could be a really interesting journey for you.

I know I'm not really there beside you, but in my heart it feels like I am. Think of me as the friend who's across the table from you at the local coffeehouse, just here to talk and process and think with you as you walk this road toward your most courageous self. I'm cheering for you.

Sincerely,

Annie

WHAT IS BRAVE?

"For I am the LORD your God who takes hold of your right
hand and says to you, Do not fear; I will help you."

—ISAIAH 41:13 NIV

*B*eing brave isn't something that happens when you're not scared
anymore. Brave people don't stop hearing the whispers of fear.
They hear the whispers but take action anyway. Being brave is
hearing that voice of fear in your head but saying, "Okay, but the truth
is, God made me on purpose and for a purpose."

Why do you want to be brave?

....

....

....

....

....

....

....

....

....

For the next one hundred days, I want to show you that you are braver than you know.

....

....

....

....

....

....

....

....

....

....

Being brave is organic and spiritual and a unique journey for each person.

Day 2

>>>>

WHY BE BRAVE?

We can only keep on going, after all, by the power of God, who first saved us and then called us to this holy work. We had nothing to do with it. It was all *his* idea, a gift prepared for us in Jesus long before we knew anything about it. But we know it now.

—2 Timothy 1:8–9 msg

It is scary to be who you're meant to be. It doesn't feel easy, because it's not. But we were made for this. Like today's scripture says, we have holy work. Why be brave? Because when we're brave enough to share the God stories in our lives, it changes the people around us. It changes us to share them.

What's your God story? How has God changed you and the circumstances of your life for the better?

....

....

....

....

....

....

> *We have to be brave so that others will be inspired to be brave along with us.*

....

....

....

....

....

....

....

....

....

....

....

Seeing other people be brave makes us want to be brave too. It's a domino effect.

Day 3

>>>> ———→

YOU ARE BRAVER
THAN YOU KNOW

*Whether you turn to the right or to the left, your ears will hear
a voice behind you, saying, "This is the way; walk in it."*

—Isaiah 30:21 NIV

If you and I sat down and you told me your story, I would be able to
show you places where you made brave choices, even if you don't
label them that way. You're probably already doing more than you
realize. You are braver than you know.

For me, day after day, I just did the next thing, took the next step,
said the next yes. I may not have felt brave, but I was taking brave steps
in obedience to God.

What brave steps have you already taken in obedience to God?

....

....

....

....

....

....

Friend, you need to know this. I never felt brave. I just did the next thing.

....

....

....

....

....

....

....

....

....

....

You are braver than you know.

Day 4

LOOK FOR BRAVE

The officials were amazed to see how brave Peter and John were, and they knew that these two apostles were only ordinary men and not well educated. The officials were certain that these men had been with Jesus.

—ACTS 4:13 CEV

There is something superpowerful about putting brave on display—in your life, in the lives of the people you love, in the art you see or read or hear. When we see brave out in the world, it inspires us, doesn't it? I think that's why we not only need to share our brave, but we need to actively look for it as well.

Is there a book, movie, song, or quote that makes you feel brave? Why does it make you feel that way?

....

....

....

....

....

....

....

....

....

When you hear other stories, they will sound like your story, and you will realize you are braver than you give yourself credit for.

....

....

....

....

....

....

....

....

....

Where do you see brave moments in your own life?

Day 5

>>>>>————→

JUST START

Saul said to David, "Go, and the LORD be with you."

—1 SAMUEL 17:37 NIV

To start the journey toward that thing—I don't know what it is for you—is not a journey *to* courage. The moment you take that first step, the moment you start, little seeds of courage, the ones I believe are already planted there right now, begin to sprout in your heart.

What are you journeying toward? Maybe it's something you long to create, write, say, or do. Take a few minutes to write about it.

....

....

....

....

....

....

....

....

....

....

....

....

....

....

....

....

....

....

....

....

You aren't headed out to find courage. It's in you; it is blooming.

Courage is with you as you say yes to things that seem scary.

Day 6

>>>> ————

THE LIES YOU BELIEVE

And the woman said to the serpent, "We may eat of the fruit of the trees in the garden, but God said, 'You shall not eat of the fruit of the tree that is in the midst of the garden, neither shall you touch it, lest you die.'" But the serpent said to the woman, "You will not surely die."

—GENESIS 3:2–4 ESV

*Y*ou hear a lie, you treat it like truth, and it begins to define you, like a label. And then you act out of that label. It's a vicious cycle that can be treated only by a heaping dose of truth—the real stuff. That's why I love the Bible. In His Word, God has already given you all the labels you need, and that's how we learn how to treat ourselves and each other.

———

Read the God-given labels below and the scriptures for each one. Find another God-give label in the Bible and add it to the list. What do these labels mean to you?

- Chosen (1 Peter 2:9)
- Forgiven (Colossians 1:13–14)
- Loved (John 3:16)
- Saved (Ephesians 2:8–9)

....

....

....

....

It's time to stop listening to Satan's lies and labels so you can hear the truth.

....

....

....

....

....

....

....

....

....

....

God has already given you all the labels you need.

— 13 —

Day 7

THE TRUTH THAT SETS YOU FREE

Jesus answered, "It is written: 'Man shall not live on bread alone, but on every word that comes from the mouth of God.'"

—MATTHEW 4:4 NIV

There is so much power when you begin to understand that you are who God says you are, not who other people say you are or who you believe you are. And believing God's truth is always a choice. In every situation, in every conversation, and in every moment that you begin to criticize yourself, you have the choice to fight for truth or give in to the lies.

What lie about yourself are you wrestling with right now? How does that lie keep you from feeling brave?

....

....

....

....

....

....

....

....

....

....

....

....

....

....

....

....

> *My insecurities are quieter, my worries are lighter, and my heart is fuller because I know how God feels about me.*

The truth that sets you free is God's Word.

Day 8

>>>>> ————

YOU AREN'T A MISTAKE

I praise you, for I am fearfully and wonderfully made.
Wonderful are your works; my soul knows it very well.

—Psalm 139:14 esv

I believe in the me God made and in the me God can make. I believe
He made me on purpose and didn't make any mistakes when it
came to my creation. That makes me feel brave. And that is the
place where I find my courage—knowing that while I am making mistakes, I am not a mistake. That is where you can find your courage too.

*Describe the you that God made. What are your best qualities? What
are your talents and abilities?*

....

....

....

....

....

....

....

....

....

We can be confident in how God made us because His Word says we are fearfully and wonderfully made.

....

....

....

....

....

....

....

....

....

....

God doesn't make mistakes.

Day 9

YOUR HEART

But you, Lord, are a compassionate and gracious God, slow to anger, abounding in love and faithfulness.

—PSALM 86:15 NIV

*A*llow God into your heart. Let Him into those little places inside that are hurt and alone and afraid. Let Him love you, lead you, and make you into the courageous person He has planned—because I promise that the adventure will be the greatest of your life.

Part of letting God love you is letting Him know you. Talk honestly with Him about your hurts, fears, dreams, and desires.

....

....

....

....

> *Our God is full of love for you—no matter what you have done or where you have been.*

....

....

....

....

....

....

....

....

....

....

God loves to love you.

Day 10

>>>>

YOUR FEET

Whoever says he abides in him ought to walk in the same way
in which he walked.

—1 John 2:6 esv

One of the truest ways to glorify God with your feet is to lead.
Lead people toward an abundant life and toward a real relationship with a real God. Lead people away from sin and choices that
cause pain. Lead people with the way you live.

*Everyone leads someone. Make a list of those who may look to you as a
leader. How can you lead them toward an abundant life?*

....

....

....

....

....

....

> *No matter how you're wired, using your feet to lead people takes bravery.*

Let your feet lead you down the path God has for you.

Day 11

YOUR MIND

Don't be like the people of this world, but let God change the
way you think. Then you will know how to do everything that
is good and pleasing to him.

—Romans 12:2 CEV

Your mind is a container, but it's a fragile container. So being
brave means taking measures to protect it. What are the portals
to your mind? Your eyes. Your ears. Those are the places you
need to guard. What you hear and what you see will affect your brain
(and heart) greatly.

How can you daily protect the portals of your mind?

....

....

....

....

....

....

....

....

Everything in the body depends on the working of the mind.

....

....

....

....

....

....

....

....

....

....

....

Be brave enough to protect your mind.

Day 12

>>>>------→

SPEAK KINDLY
TO YOURSELF

The tongue has the power of life and death, and those who
love it will eat its fruit.

—PROVERBS 18:21 NIV

Friend, stop being mean to yourself. Seriously. If you are going to
be the person who does the brave things God is calling you to do,
speaking life and developing beautiful things in others with your
words, it begins with doing that for yourself. Kind words have power,
and if you believe them, you will be brave.

---

*Does the majority of your self-talk build you up or leave you feeling
unloved and afraid? Write down three kind things to say to yourself,
then say them out loud in front of a mirror.*

....

....

....

....

....

....

Speak kindly to yourself, as Jesus speaks kindly to you.

....

....

....

....

....

....

....

....

....

....

....

....

Speaking kindly to yourself will make you brave.

Day 13

>>> ———

LIKE WHAT YOU LIKE

For the Spirit God gave us does not make us timid, but gives us
power, love and self-discipline.

—2 Timothy 1:7 niv

You know what's brave? Giving yourself permission to do the
thing you want to do, to like whatever *you* want to like. That's
my hope for you. That as you grow to love yourself more and
more, you will feel brave enough to love the things you love instead of
altering them because you think that's what it will take to be accepted.

*What do you really like? What's your favorite way to relax? What type
of music do you feel connected to? What TV show character makes you
feel strong enough to be yourself? Make a list of all your favorites.*

....

....

....

....

....

....

....

....

> You are accepted by God. And hopefully you accept you too.

....

....

....

....

....

....

....

....

....

....

....

You can like anything you want to like.

Day 14

>>>> ———→

GOD MADE YOU
ON PURPOSE

The LORD will fulfill his purpose for me; your steadfast love,
O LORD, endures forever. Do not forsake the work of your
hands.

—PSALM 138:8 ESV

God made you once. You were worth the work that first time.
Then He threw away that mold because one of you is enough for
Him. You're enough. You are the sacred painting, the original.
God made us this way on purpose, and He created us for His glory.
We were made especially by God to promote Him, glorify Him, and
worship Him.

*List a few ways you—unique, original, one-of-a-kind you—can live for
God's glory this week.*

....

....

....

....

....

....

....

....

....

....

....

....

....

....

....

....

When God made you, He did something that only He can do, and He did that for His glory.

Your call to courage is as unique as you are.

Day 15

>>>> ————→

ASK THE HARD
QUESTIONS

"Call to me and I will answer you and tell you great and
unsearchable things you do not know."

—JEREMIAH 33:3 NIV

It takes bravery to ask the hard questions and listen for hard answers.
But whatever it is, you can ask. Even if and when things are hard,
you can always ask God, *What's Your plan for me? What am I
supposed to be learning right now?* He will show you the answer. And
those answers, my friend? They are the answers that bring peace.

What hard question is on your heart right now?

....

....

....

....

....

....

....

....

....

....

> *Knowing that God works for your good and that His answers can be trusted is a great remedy for fear.*

....

....

....

....

....

....

....

....

....

....

....

Don't be afraid to ask God the things you really want to know.

Day 16

BELIEVE YOU ARE NEVER ALONE

"And surely I am with you always, to the very end of the age."

—MATTHEW 28:20 NIV

Do you know what *Immanuel* means? It is one of God's names, and it means "God with us." Because Jesus paid the price for our sin, God is always with us. See? Even when you feel alone, you actually aren't. He is the One who sticks with you no matter what. And you are brave enough to believe that what He said is true. He is always with you.

What hard thing is God leading you to do? Is the fear of doing it alone holding you back?

....

....

....

....

....

....

....

....

....

....

....

....

....

....

....

Do the hard thing God is leading you to do. You are never alone.

Jesus said He would be with us until the end of time.

Day 17

>>>>

DIG INTO THE WORD
FOR YOURSELF

Every part of Scripture is God-breathed and useful one way or another—showing us truth, exposing our rebellion, correcting our mistakes, training us to live God's way. Through the Word we are put together and shaped up for the tasks God has for us.

—2 TIMOTHY 3:16–17 MSG

The Bible is always your best resource when you want to hear from God. There, in black and white (and sometimes red), are God-inspired words for you. Don't rely on your pastor, a podcast, or even a Christian author to read a few verses here and there. Dig into the Word for yourself, and enjoy this gift God has given you—total access to who He is and total knowledge of how He feels about you!

How do you feel about the Bible? Does it inspire you, confuse you, challenge you, bore you, or a mix of all of these?

....

....

....

....

....

....

The Bible is God's way of communicating with you, of letting you in on who He is.

....

....

....

....

....

....

....

....

....

....

The Bible is a record of who God is and His great love for His people.

Day 18

>>>———→

PRAY

This is the confidence we have in approaching God: that if we
ask anything according to his will, he hears us.

—1 John 5:14 niv

*A*re you brave enough to pray and believe that God hears you
and changes things? Are you brave enough to believe with your
whole heart that God will do something miraculous? Are you
brave enough to say the first words to Him after you've been silent for a
while? Prayer isn't about us, really. Prayer is this amazing opportunity
to connect directly with the greatest Being who has always been.

*What is something you want changed? Take your desire to God, and
be brave enough to believe He can do anything, even what seems
impossible.*

....

....

....

....

....

....

....

God is absolutely real. And He is listening.

....

....

....

....

....

....

....

....

....

....

....

....

It takes courage to connect with God through prayer.

Day 19

>>> →

HAVE FAITH

Now faith is confidence in what we hope for and assurance about what we do not see.

—HEBREWS 11:1 NIV

When Satan pushes your buttons or makes you doubt God's Word or God's love for you, what's your first brave move? Hold up the shield of faith that you hold over your heart. Just believe. It isn't always easy—in fact it rarely is, but the good stuff is never cheap. And what happens to your soul on the other side of a fight for faith is the good stuff.

When was a time you had to fight for your faith? How did you grow in that season?

....

....

....

....

....

> *Ask God to fill you with faith—faith in Him, faith in His promises, faith in His ways.*

When you ask God to increase your faith, He will.

Day 20

GOD IS WHO HE SAYS HE IS

God is not human, that he should lie, not a human being, that he should change his mind. Does he speak and then not act? Does he promise and not fulfill?

—NUMBERS 23:19 NIV

You are deeply loved and called to be courageous by a God who is perfect and perfectly trustworthy. If you feel stuck looking at your own shortcomings, look upward to your Jesus, who is exactly who He says He is, who defeated death itself, and who empowers you to be brave.

Romans 8:11 says you are empowered by the same Spirit who lived in Jesus. How does that help you to feel brave?

....

....

....

....

....

....

....

....

Instead of looking at yourself and your own abilities, look at God and believe that He is who He says He is.

....

....

....

....

....

....

....

....

....

....

God is making you brave day by day.

Day 21

>>> ————

YOU CAN HEAR GOD

"The shepherd walks right up to the gate. The gatekeeper opens the gate to him and the sheep recognize his voice. He calls his own sheep by name and leads them out. When he gets them all out, he leads them and they follow because they are familiar with his voice."

—JOHN 10:2–4 MSG

I strongly disagree with the people who say God doesn't speak to us anymore. I think He is always speaking to us—through the Bible, through nature, through others, through Jesus' life, and directly through the Holy Spirit who lives in us. You can hear Him too, if you want to. He's speaking, and He will talk to you if you're listening.

What do you want to hear from God right now? Are you seeking guidance, direction, comfort, or something else?

....

....

....

....

....

....

....

> *I have learned to hear God's voice in my life. I know that quiet voice and that gentle push.*

....

....

....

....

....

....

....

....

....

....

....

Take a deep breath and learn to hear God's voice in your life.

Day 22

>>> ———→

YOU ARE WHO GOD
SAYS YOU ARE

Therefore, as God's chosen people, holy and dearly loved, clothe yourselves with compassion, kindness, humility, gentleness and patience.

—Colossians 3:12 NIV

When you spend time with God and immerse yourself in the truth of His Word, you will easily notice the lies and the things you hear in your head that aren't really you. You will hear the truth of who God says you are much more clearly, like how you are dearly loved.

Who does God say you are?

....

....

....

....

....

....

....

....

All over His Word, God says that you are strong and important on this planet.

....

....

....

....

....

....

....

....

....

....

....

You are accepted. You are secure. You can be brave.

Day 23

BELIEVE GOD CARES ABOUT YOUR DREAMS

"If you, then, though you are evil, know how to give good gifts to your children, how much more will your Father in heaven give good gifts to those who ask him!"

—MATTHEW 7:11 NIV

I think there is something really powerful about being smack in the middle of an unwanted season and being able to look yourself right in the eyeball and say, "God has not forgotten you. Your life and your dreams are important to God." So share your dreams with your Father, who loves you and loves to give you good gifts.

What good gifts has God already given you? What do you want that you don't yet have?

. . . .

. . . .

. . . .

....

....

....

....

God hears us when we pray. He cares about you, and He cares about your dreams.

....

....

....

....

....

....

....

....

....

....

Dream and believe that God is working in those dreams.

Day 24

>>>> ————

DREAM BIG

And while [Jesus] was at Bethany in the house of Simon the leper, as he was reclining at table, a woman came with an alabaster flask of ointment of pure nard, very costly, and she broke the flask and poured it over his head. There were some who said to themselves indignantly, "Why was the ointment wasted like that? For this ointment could have been sold for more than three hundred denarii and given to the poor." And they scolded her. But Jesus said, "Leave her alone. Why do you trouble her? She has done a beautiful thing to me."

—MARK 14:3–6 ESV

*D*ream big. Be brave enough to believe that as much as you could want, God could give to you. We are meant to make a big impact on the planet. Bigger than we could ever dream up on our own. It still amazes me how God's dream for me was so much greater than the one I'd been planning all along.

Name someone who's doing big things for God. What impresses you about his or her story? What's a big thing you want to do for God?

....

....

....

God's dream for me was so much greater.

....

....

....

....

....

....

....

....

....

....

....

Be brave enough to dream big.

Day 25

>>>> ──────

DREAM IN PIECES

The LORD who rescued me from the paw of the lion and the
paw of the bear will rescue me from the hand of this Philistine.

—1 SAMUEL 17:37 NIV

*G*od knows we need dreams in pieces because we would be
too scared of the whole puzzle. Had I known I'd be an author
and a speaker back when I was in college, I probably would
have crawled under my covers and stayed there for a year or five. I'm
here today because of the little steps and the brave moments dotted
throughout my writing career that have grown into this.

*What little steps of bravery have you already taken toward your
dream? What's the next step?*

....

....

....

....

....

....

....

....

Daily steps of courage lead to the bigger story.

....

....

....

....

....

....

....

....

....

....

....

Believe in who God is and that God has a role
for you to play that will require courage.

Day 26

>>>> ———→

WHAT'S AN OPEN DOOR?

He leads me in paths of righteousness for his name's sake.

—PSALM 23:3 ESV

When I was a sophomore in college, I knew I wanted to go on a mission trip, and the one to Scotland stood out to me. It wasn't superspiritual. It was an open door. Going on a trip overseas, and later to live there, took courage. It was different. It was new. And I wasn't following a path lit with bright arrows. It was an open door that God led me through. Ask the Lord to lead *you* to the open doors, then be brave enough to walk through them.

When has God opened a door for you? What came of that opportunity? What door would you like to see Him open for you now?

....

....

....

....

....

....

....

....

How do you know when to make a brave move, even if it isn't easy?

....

....

....

....

....

....

....

....

....

....

....

....

Ask God to show you the open doors in your life right now.

Day 27

WHAT'S A CLOSED DOOR?

Commit to the LORD whatever you do, and he will establish your plans.

—PROVERBS 16:3 NIV

Brave people commit their work to the Lord and trust that His plan for their lives might not look the way they planned. If you're looking at a closed door today, then there's an open one just around the corner. Be brave enough to walk through the doors that the Lord leads you through. Even when they are unexpected or feel scary.

When has God closed a door for you? What came of it—did you adjust your plan or wait for an open door?

....

....

....

....

....

> *Closed doors can be confusing. But when they happen, you can be brave.*

You can be brave because you can trust God.

Day 28

MOURN DREAMS
THAT HAVE DIED

My soul melts away for sorrow; strengthen me according to your word!

—Psalm 119:28 esv

It's easy to take the unanswered prayers and disappointments in our lives and brush them under the rug so we don't have to think about them. Looking at those dreams takes bravery. But when you look them in the face, head-on, and let them go, you will see how God's plan for your life, although different from what you expected, is a beautiful story of its own.

What unanswered prayer or lost dream have you faced?

....

....

....

....

....

....

....

It's okay to mourn your dreams that have died.

....

....

....

....

....

....

....

....

....

....

....

If you saw a life for yourself that you will never have, mourn that loss.

Day 29

>>>> ———

CHASE THE DREAMS
THAT ARE ALIVE

The purposes of a person's heart are deep waters, but one who
has insight draws them out.

—Proverbs 20:5 niv

have friends who are sure that life has passed them by, that their
opportunity to be brave has come and gone. That is sadder to me
than anything—you are not too old! If you're reading this, you're
alive, and if you're alive, so is a dream. And God wants to take your
dreams and talents and use them to point others to Him.

_What dreams did you have as a child? Are any of those dreams still
alive in your heart today?_

....

....

....

....

> *Sometimes being brave is walking away from the dreams that have died and the doors that have closed and chasing the dreams that are alive.*

God loves to put wings on dreams that His kids chase, dreams that can bring Him glory.

Day 30

TELL SOMEONE

And let us consider how we may spur one another on toward love and good deeds, not giving up meeting together, as some are in the habit of doing, but encouraging one another—and all the more as you see the Day approaching.

—HEBREWS 10:24–25 NIV

At my home church one year, I helped high school students host and run the middle school retreat. One night, Mallory, who was just a few months from heading off to Auburn University, woke me up to talk.

"I don't want to go to Auburn. I think," she stammered slowly, "I want to be a missionary."

"Okay, Mal. You can do that."

Mallory didn't begin her journey toward courage right there. That little glow of courage had been growing in her heart for days, maybe weeks. And then it grew feet, didn't it? Feet that led her to tell someone.

Think about a dream (maybe there's more than one) alive in you today. What questions or fears do you have? What obstacles stand in your way? Who can you tell about this dream?

....

....

....

Tell somebody you want to be brave, and then see what God can do.

....

....

....

....

....

....

....

....

....

....

Do you want to be brave? Tell someone.

Day 31

>>>> ───────

HOW DO YOU FIND THE PEOPLE TO TELL?

Without good direction, people lose their way; the more wise counsel you follow, the better your chances.

—PROVERBS 11:14 MSG

When it comes to your dreams, you need to guard your heart. Your heart is precious, your dreams should be shared with only a few close friends, and you should love well but carefully. You need to allow love into your heart, but always remember to guard and protect it.

────────────

Choose two or three people you trust and could continually reach out to as you pursue your dream. Do you have a time set up to meet with one of these friends? Have you already met? How did it go?

....

....

....

_____

_____

_____

_____

> *Wise people live wise lives. Find them. Watch for them. And then keep them around your life.*

_____

_____

_____

_____

_____

_____

_____

_____

Share your dream with someone who has pursued his or her dream and achieved it and someone who mourned a dream and moved on to another one.

>>>> ———

THE DIFFERENCE
BETWEEN DREAMS
AND CALLING

God's gifts and God's call are under full warranty—never canceled, never rescinded.

—ROMANS 11:29 MSG

Dreams are different from your calling. Your calling is sure and strong. Your calling, the thing that God has placed in you for the good of the planet and the good of your heart, isn't going anywhere. Your dreams will change over time. Some will come to pass, and some will pass away. But your calling will remain true.

How would you describe your calling?

....

....

....

....

....

....

> *Build your life
> around your calling,
> not your dreams.*

....

....

....

....

....

....

....

....

....

....

....

*Your calling is the ingredient in the kitchen;
your dreams are all the ways you use it.*

>>>> ———

WHAT ARE YOU
CREATED TO DO?

I want you to think about how all this makes you more
significant, not less. A body isn't just a single part blown up
into something huge. It's all the different-but-similar parts
arranged and functioning together.

—1 Corinthians 12:14 msg

How do you know what you were created to do? We know, as
Christians, that we are all called to point people to Christ. But
how are you supposed to do that practically, using your unique
makeup? Ask God. Spend time in His Word. God is always speaking
to us.

What has God helped you to understand about why He created you?
Ask Him now to show you how to live out your calling, then wait,
listen, and journal what you hear.

. . . .

. . . .

....

....

....

God is the One who decided what your role in the body would be.

....

....

....

....

....

....

....

....

....

....

....

The best way to grow in your ability to hear God is to practice and let others help you.

Day 34

>>>>

ONE CALLING

There are different kinds of spiritual gifts, but they all come from the same Spirit. There are different ways to serve the same Lord, and we can each do different things. Yet the same God works in all of us and helps us in everything we do.

—1 CORINTHIANS 12:4–6 CEV

*J*obs will come and go. Your calling won't, whether it's parenting or mentoring, teaching, nursing, building. It's not what you do but how you do it. So don't be afraid to try out a different expression of your calling. Don't let fear of failure keep you from what God wants you to do.

What are some ways you've expressed your calling in the past? What are some ways you dream about expressing your calling in the future?

....

....

....

....

....

....

....

Each of our lives has a thesis statement—a main thing—one calling.

....

....

....

....

....

....

....

....

....

....

....

....

Ask God to help you find the ways you express your calling.

Day 35

>>>>

MULTIPLE EXPRESSIONS

With my whole heart I seek you; let me not wander from your commandments!

—PSALM 119:10 ESV

Maybe you've taken the last few days to figure out your calling. Maybe God has given you a clear picture and you're exploring what that looks like in your life. As you sort through this with the Lord, don't listen to the enemy when he tries to discourage you. Hear this—you are not too old to figure out your calling, and you're not too young to have already had multiple expressions of it.

What next step must you take to explore a new expression of your calling?

....

....

....

....

....

....

....

....

....

One calling.
Multiple
expressions.
Be brave and
explore them.

....

....

....

....

....

....

....

....

....

....

We all have one calling, but it can be expressed in lots of ways.

Day 36

WORK IN PIECES

The plans of the diligent lead surely to abundance, but everyone who is hasty comes only to poverty.

—Proverbs 21:5 ESV

What should you do today? Do what's right in front of you. If your dream is to someday be the president of your company, don't show up late to work every day now as an employee. Do your best today, in whatever spot or position you're in. That will take you to the next piece.

What piece of your calling is in front of you today? What can you do to make the most of the work in front of you now?

....

....

....

....

....

....

....

....

....

....

....

....

....

....

....

....

....

....

....

> *Be brave enough to work where you are.*

To enjoy the fruit of working out of your calling,
work hard on one piece at a time.

Day 37

>>>>

WHERE CAN YOUR
CALLING TAKE YOU?

God can do anything, you know—far more than you could
ever imagine or guess or request in your wildest dreams! He
does it not by pushing us around but by working within us, his
Spirit deeply and gently within us.

—Ephesians 3:20 MSG

Where can your calling take you? It's unlimited! If you're not
sure what this looks like for you, be brave enough to sit
some people down and say, "Hey. Help me, please?" What's
cool about your calling is that there are no dead ends. Even if you
weren't brave enough to pursue your last opportunity, you can be brave
this time.

*Where can your calling take you? If you aren't sure, reach out to one of
your supporters and ask for prayer over your next steps.*

....

....

....

....

> *God knows where your calling will take you, and if you're brave, soon you will too.*

....

....

....

....

....

....

....

....

....

....

Inviting people to help you can feel scary,
but be brave enough to listen.

Day 38

>>>> ─────────→

WHEN YOUR CALLING
ISN'T YOUR JOB

Whatever you do, work heartily, as for the Lord and not for
men.

—COLOSSIANS 3:23 ESV

There are times when you're doing a job that is not your calling.
Maybe you feel like every hour that you work at your job, you're
doing the opposite of your calling. You've got to be brave enough
to be faithful, even when you don't want to be. You've got to be brave
to work hard now for a payoff that won't come until later. But it is so
worth it!

*Even if your current job isn't what you'd pick, what are some ways you
can give your all to it? What experience or important lessons can you
learn from it?*

....

....

....

....

....

....

....

....

....

....

....

....

....

....

....

....

....

....

I never would have been able to make it, doing what I love, if I hadn't worked hard at the jobs that weren't my calling.

Hardly anyone goes from discovering their calling to getting their perfect dream job.

Day 39

>»»>> ———— →

FIND YOUR CALLING
AT YOUR JOB

Therefore, my dear brothers and sisters, stand firm. Let
nothing move you. Always give yourselves fully to the work
of the Lord, because you know that your labor in the Lord is
not in vain.

—1 Corinthians 15:58 niv

Let's say your dream is to be a nurse. Are you brave enough to say,
"I've always dreamed of being a nurse because I love taking care of
people. And here I am working at a restaurant. But, hey, I still can
take care of people"? Can you look around at the life you have and find
ways that your calling is already there, even if your job doesn't look the
way you thought it would look?

What piece of your calling can you find in what you're doing now?

....

....

....

....

....

....

Are you brave enough to find your calling at your not-quite-it job?

....

....

....

....

....

....

....

....

....

....

....

....

You can be brave and find your calling no matter what your job is now.

Day 40

>>>>

WORK HARD

Hard work always pays off; mere talk puts no bread on the table.

—Proverbs 14:23 MSG

You gain a lot when you work really hard. You gain respect. You get to keep your job. You gain a good reputation. It isn't always fun, but don't you want to be a person who is known for working hard? Whatever you're doing and whatever you're asked to do, work hard. It really does pay off.

What are small things you can do every day to gain a good reputation at your job?

....

....

....

....

....

> *Persevere. Work hard. Don't be wimpy.*

Work hard today, friend, and see what comes from it.

Day 41

>>> ———

WHO YOU DO LIFE WITH
MATTERS AS MUCH
AS WHAT YOU DO

As iron sharpens iron, so one person sharpens another.

—Proverbs 27:17 NIV

We've got to be brave enough to find balance. Even if there's financial pressure (there usually is, isn't there?). Even if there's pressure at work. We have to be brave enough to balance work and life because we need relationships. Share your life with others.

Think about your people. What kind of influence do they have on your life?

....

....

....

....

....

....

....

....

....

Don't let pursuing your dreams or maximizing your calling keep you from investing in relationships.

....

....

....

....

....

....

....

....

....

....

When you're going after your calling, don't
abandon the people who matter.

Day 42

BRAVE PEOPLE NEED PEOPLE

You are better off to have a friend than to be all alone, because then you will get more enjoyment out of what you earn. If you fall, your friend can help you up. But if you fall without having a friend nearby, you are really in trouble.

—ECCLESIASTES 4:9–10 CEV

We all need people. But it's easier to have a relationship with your Netflix queue. Why? Because you don't have to say any painful good-byes. You don't have any friction with your Netflix shows. If you don't like a show, you drop it. But friendship takes work. Friendship takes courage. You've got to be brave and let yourself love people.

What relationships in your life have already proven to be worth the effort? Who can you invest more time in?

> To make brave
> choices, you have
> got to have support.

As hard as relationships can be, we wouldn't trade them for the world.

Day 43

YOUR FAMILY

Long, long ago he decided to adopt us into his family through Jesus Christ. (What pleasure he took in planning this!) He wanted us to enter into the celebration of his lavish gift-giving by the hand of his beloved Son.

—Ephesians 1:5–6 msg

Being brave in your family means loving your family well even if your family isn't always healthy. It's following the example of God, who lives and breathes forgiveness and grace. It's asking Him for wisdom with those in your family who baffle you. Pray for the courage to stick with your family and love them as they are, the way God has loved you.

How have you had to be brave in your family? What's the healthiest way to love your family?

....

....

....

....

....

....

....

....

For many people, loving your family can take more courage than any of your other relationships combined.

....

....

....

....

....

....

....

....

....

....

Are you brave enough to build a family even if you had problems in your nuclear family?

Day 44

>>>>———

YOUR FRIENDS

Love one another with brotherly affection. Outdo one another
in showing honor.

—ROMANS 12:10 ESV

I know I sound like a broken record about this, but *you need friends*.
They need you. You need to be brave and let people get close enough
to speak into your life. The gift of community is so sweet, but you
have to be brave and let down your defenses to develop those relationships in your life.

What defenses are keeping you from developing closer relationships?

....

....

....

....

....

....

I'm so thankful my friends were brave enough to let me into their lives and that I was brave enough to let them into mine.

Love will change you. It will change your friends.

Day 45

DATING AND MARRIAGE

Trust GOD from the bottom of your heart; don't try to figure out everything on your own. Listen for GOD's voice in everything you do, everywhere you go; he's the one who will keep you on track.

—PROVERBS 3:5–6 MSG

f you're not married yet but want to be, go on dates. Seriously. Put yourself out there, friend. You just have to go for it, even when it's scary or unknown.

Married friends, keep being brave in your marriage. Give your spouse grace. Be brave enough to be open and communicate your feelings. Don't let the years of hurts and pain put a wall between you. Don't run away when you feel rejected.

If you're single but want to get married someday, what's the biggest obstacle you face in dating? If you're married, what's the biggest obstacle you face in maintaining a healthy marriage?

....

....

....

....

....

....

....

....

....

....

....

....

....

....

You will learn things about God's love and personality from friendship, dating, and marriage.

Fear will try to keep you from giving your heart
in relationships. Don't let fear win.

Day 46

>>>———→

YOUR CHURCH

Love is patient and kind; love does not envy or boast; it is
not arrogant or rude. It does not insist on its own way; it is
not irritable or resentful; it does not rejoice at wrongdoing,
but rejoices with the truth. Love bears all things, believes all
things, hopes all things, endures all things.

—1 Corinthians 13:4–7 esv

Brave Christians get plugged in to their church. But just like any
relationship, you and the church will have rocky times. Just like
any relationship, at some point the flawed humans who lead your
church will disappoint you, and you will need to put 1 Corinthians 13
love into action. Brave people are willing to stay plugged in, even when
things get hard.

———————————

Are you plugged in to a church? If you're not, what's holding you back?
If you are, describe how you feel about it.

....

....

....

_____

_____

_____

_____

> *If we unplug from our church, we're unplugging from our support system.*

_____

_____

_____

_____

_____

_____

_____

_____

_____

_____

_____

*Church gives us the opportunity to wrestle
inside so that we can love well outside.*

Day 47

>>>>

FIND A MENTOR

Walk with the wise and become wise, for a companion of fools suffers harm.

—Proverbs 13:20 NIV

*F*inding a mentor seems like a scary thought, but it's really not. I'll make it really simple for you. Find someone you respect in your life who is two or three steps ahead of you, someone you can go to dinner with and ask the hard questions. Invite people in and learn from their wisdom. You will reap crazy benefits from inviting mentors into your life.

What area of your life could use more guidance? Maybe with your job, relationships, church, or calling? Who could mentor you in this area?

....

....

....

....

....

....

....

....

....

It takes bravery to put yourself out there and ask someone to give you some of his or her wisdom.

....

....

....

....

....

....

....

....

....

....

....

Be brave and ask.

Day 48

YOUR ONLINE LIFE

"You are the light of the world. A city set on a hill cannot be hidden. Nor do people light a lamp and put it under a basket, but on a stand, and it gives light to all in the house. In the same way, let your light shine before others, so that they may see your good works and give glory to your Father who is in heaven."

—MATTHEW 5:14–16 ESV

The medium doesn't matter. Facebook. Twitter. Blog. Instagram. Pinterest. You have so many chances to share light, to share God, to make Him known to the people who listen to your voice. But the internet is not exactly a Christ-welcoming place. It takes courage to share your faith and be a light for Jesus, whether you're online or not.

How are you being a light for Jesus while you're online?

....

....

....

....

....

....

> *We are to be a light wherever we go, even online.*

....

....

....

....

....

....

....

....

....

....

....

We need to view technology as tools God gave us to glorify Him.

Day 49

>>>> ————

YOUR WORDS MATTER

In the beginning, God created the heavens and the earth. The earth was without form and void, and darkness was over the face of the deep. And the Spirit of God was hovering over the face of the waters. And God said, "Let there be light," and there was light.

—Genesis 1:1–3 ESV

Proverbs 18:21 tells us that our tongues have the power of life and death. I see that in my life. I see that in my friendships. I see that in the memories of past things said to me. Words matter. God wants you to use your words to encourage and speak life. Ask Him for the grace to do so, and look for opportunities to be brave, speaking truth and love into a broken world.

Write down some of the encouraging things others have said to you. How do those words help you to feel brave?

....

....

....

....

....

....

....

....

....

If there are seeds of courage living in all of us, waiting to bloom, words are the sun and the water that cheer on those seeds to their fullness.

....

....

....

....

....

....

....

....

Encouraging words give you the push you need.

Day 50

>>>> ————

WHEN RELATIONSHIPS CHANGE

I lift up my eyes to the mountains—where does my help come from? My help comes from the LORD, the Maker of heaven and earth.

—PSALM 121:1–2 NIV

What do you do when things are broken with your person? You lift your eyes up to your Helper. Your Comforter. Your Father. Your Friend. Jesus cares and understands. He allowed His relationship with His Father to be broken for you. If your relationship is changing in a way that is heartbreaking, don't try to distract the pain away. Be brave enough to let Jesus into the ripped places.

What relationship do you see going through a change? How do you feel about it? Is there anything you can do to mend the relationship?

....

....

....

....

....

....

....

....

Every relationship changes. That's a hard reality, one that absolutely requires me to lift my eyes up and let the Lord help.

....

....

....

....

....

....

....

....

....

....

When a relationship changes, let the Lord help you through it.

Day 51

>>>>

CHANGE ALWAYS HAPPENS

Every good and perfect gift is from above, coming down from the Father of the heavenly lights, who does not change like shifting shadows.

—James 1:17 niv

I f I chose to live in a world where I hated change all the time, I would be really miserable. If I chose to put all my hope in people, I would be really miserable. (I've tried both. It's always miserable.) I don't love change, but I know that God is always working for my good. So remember that He's the boss and that He loves us. That can make us brave, even when everything that felt secure seems to be changing.

What changes in your life are you dreading right now? What changes are you excited about? How is God using these changes to shape you?

....

....

....

....

....

....

> *Brave people are willing to let go of everything as they hold tight to God.*

....

....

....

....

....

....

....

....

....

....

....

You have a totally trustworthy God who is looking out for you.

Day 52

PREPARE FOR CHANGE

Jesus Christ is the same yesterday and today and forever.

—HEBREWS 13:8 NIV

We can be brave because Jesus is constant, even when our circumstances are not. I need that reminder—that just as the seasons change on earth, they are going to change in my life. And when I start to sense that little bit of shift, like the first hints of fall, I have to prepare and see it coming and know it's all part of the journey.

What can you do to prepare for the changes you see coming in the next few days, weeks, or months?

....

....

....

....

....

....

....

....

How do you prepare for change? Spend time talking to the unchanging One.

....

....

....

....

....

....

....

....

....

....

....

....

....

Trust Him, keep your eyes on Him, and let the seasons change.

Day 53

>>>>———

SMALL DECISIONS MATTER

What a person plants, he will harvest.

—GALATIANS 6:7 MSG

S mall decisions don't feel very brave in the moment. When you think of being brave, you probably think of giant leaps. Grand gestures. Those are clearly brave. But it's also brave to be intentional to make small, healthy decisions because it goes against our human nature to put effort into things that are seemingly insignificant.

Name a small decision you can make today that will lead toward your dream, your desired job, or the way you'd like to express your calling.

....

....

....

....

....

....

....

....

....

....

....

....

....

....

....

....

....

....

....

....

....

It's brave to make small decisions with the big picture in mind.

A little yes can be a step in the right direction, even if it isn't a leap.

Day 54

>>>>

SAY YES

The righteous are as bold as a lion.

—Proverbs 28:1 NIV

If the yeses feel scary, take comfort in knowing that if you are seeking God, if you are asking Him to lead you, He hears you and is doing just that! If you are living in obedience to Him, and He brings opportunities into your life, you can trust that He will take care of you when you say yes.

It's often hardest to say yes when something is new. What's something new you can say yes to this week? (It doesn't have to be big—try a new restaurant, say yes to that invitation, or explore a new way to serve.)

....

....

....

....

....

....

....

....

....

....

Say yes to the situations that stretch you and scare you and ask you to be a better you than you think you can be.

....

....

....

....

....

....

....

....

....

Say yes to Jesus in every way—every chance you get.

Day 55

>>>>———————→

SAY NO

But even if he does not [rescue us], we want you to know, Your
Majesty, that we will not serve your gods or worship the image
of gold you have set up.

—Daniel 3:18 NIV

A lot of courageous nos make for some beautifully brave yeses. And
I'm not sure you are going to get it right every time—saying the
right yeses and the right nos. I don't get it right all the time. But
courage doesn't equal right; courage equals stepping out and trying.

When is it hard for you to say no?

....

....

....

....

....

....

....

....

....

....

....

....

....

....

....

....

....

....

....

....

Say the thing that courage asks you to say, even if it's the word **no.**

Be brave and say yes. But also be brave and say no.

Day 56

>>>>

IN THE WAITING SEASON

Wait for the LORD; be strong, and let your heart take courage;
wait for the LORD!

—PSALM 27:14 ESV

When we remember how patient the Lord is with us, it can help us be patient in our seasons of waiting. Waiting for our work to pay off. Waiting for a relationship to heal. Waiting for a trial to end. You can be brave in whatever type of waiting season you find yourself when you are living in total dependence on your ever-patient, ever-present Father.

Think of a waiting season from your past. When did it end? How did God show Himself faithful?

....

....

....

....

....

....

....

....

Life is full of waiting seasons, and you can brave out the wait and do it well.

....

....

....

....

....

....

....

....

....

....

....

Be brave enough to be patient, not just outwardly but inwardly.

Day 57

>>>>

WHEN YOU HOLD ON

These hard times are small potatoes compared to the coming good times, the lavish celebration prepared for us. There's far more here than meets the eye. The things we see now are here today, gone tomorrow. But the things we can't see now will last forever.

—2 CORINTHIANS 4:17–18 MSG

*D*on't let go because it hurts or because it is hard. Don't let go because you feel like it is ridiculous to hold on. It's not. Hold on until the Lord makes it really clear that you're supposed to let go. But while you are listening, persevere, and lean toward holding on until God and other people make it really clear that you're supposed to let go.

What are you struggling to hold on to right now? It could be in your heart, in life, or both.

....

....

....

....

....

....

....

....

....

....

....

....

....

....

....

....

....

Don't give up on life. Don't give up on God. Don't give up on yourself.

Hold on to hope, love.

Day 58

WHEN YOU LET GO

"Forget the former things; do not dwell on the past. See, I am doing a new thing! Now it springs up; do you not perceive it?"

—ISAIAH 43:18–19 NIV

I t may be a relationship or a job or a city or some money or old hurts. When it is time to let go, you know it. Your fingers long to ease their grip, but your heart begs them to hold on—not because it's the best for you, but because the unknown is scary. Only in letting go are your hands free to grab on to the next thing. Please let go.

Do you sense anything you should let go of now?

....

....

....

....

....

....

....

....

....

....

The deeper call for courage comes when you let go with nothing ahead to grab.

....

....

....

....

....

....

....

....

....

....

....

....

Be brave enough to empty your hands. You can trust in God!

Day 59

>>>>

WHEN CHANGE HURTS

And we know that in all things God works for the good of those who love him, who have been called according to his purpose.

—ROMANS 8:28 NIV

B rave people are okay with change because they remember that change is for our good. That doesn't mean you have to love change or seek change or want change. That doesn't mean that when something takes an unexpected turn you have to throw a party. It means that if you're brave, you can walk through change with grace and hope that God's promises are true and all things really do work together for good.

When have you seen an unwanted change work out for good? (This could be in your life or someone else's.)

....

....

....

....

....

....

....

A brave person's joy isn't dependent on circumstances. God has got this, whatever it is.

....

....

....

....

....

....

....

....

....

God wants you to live bravely in the knowledge that He is ultimately in control.

Day 60

LIFE IS HARD

"I have told you these things, so that in me you may have peace. In this world you will have trouble. But take heart! I have overcome the world."

—John 16:33 niv

Life isn't always easy. In fact, I think I'm growing to believe that life isn't often easy. So, yeah, you can be sad. You can be angry. You can be confused. But you don't ever have reason to despair. Even when it gets tragic and dark, do not despair. You are braver than that.

What difficult thoughts and feelings have you been dealing with recently? What can keep you from despair?

....

....

....

....

....

....

.... *God knows that life is painful.*

....

....

....

....

....

....

....

....

....

....

....

Tragedy can sneak up on you and send your world into a tailspin. But don't despair.

Day 61

>>>>

FAILURE IS INEVITABLE

See what kind of love the Father has given to us, that we should be called children of God; and so we are.

—1 John 3:1 esv

I'm sorry if I'm the first to tell you this, but brave or not, you *are* going to fail. Failing doesn't make you a failure. It's when we let it define us that things go wrong. Brave people don't let failure define them; they let failure teach them, knowing that God loves them no matter what.

What defines your life instead of fear or failure?

....

....

....

....

....

....

....

....

....

When you know who loves you, you know where you can go when you fail.

....

....

....

....

....

....

....

....

....

....

....

....

Brave people know that they can fail and nothing will change between them and their Father.

Day 62

DON'T BE AFRAID

"Have I not commanded you? Be strong and courageous. Do not be afraid; do not be discouraged, for the LORD your God will be with you wherever you go."

—JOSHUA 1:9 NIV

What is the big question lingering in your heart that you don't know how to answer? It could be a location change, a job change, or a relationship. If the reason you don't say yes is simply, "I'm afraid," then you need to seek the Lord and ask Him to help you be brave, and then answer the question based on what He leads you to do.

Write the big question lingering in your heart. How do you sense the Lord leading you to answer it?

....

....

....

....

....

....

When we take steps forward, we've got to say no to fear.

....

....

....

....

....

....

....

....

....

....

....

....

....

Please don't let fear win.

Day 63

>>>>──────

FACE YOUR PAIN

Even though I walk through the valley of the shadow of death,
I will fear no evil, for you are with me; your rod and your staff,
they comfort me.

—PSALM 23:4 ESV

It's better when you say the thing you're facing out loud. That's brave.
Telling someone about your pain, whether it's lies the enemy plants
in your head or a devastating circumstance you're wading through,
is brave. When you face the pain—look at it and call it what it is—you
will begin to experience healing. Hiding it doesn't lead to healing.

What pain is weighing you down right now?

....

....

....

....

....

....

....

....

....

> *Face your pain.*
> *Bring it to God.*
> *Bring it to another*
> *person and find*
> *healing there.*

....

....

....

....

....

....

....

....

....

....

Friend, are you hurting? Don't run from it.

Day 64

>>>> →

INVITE SOMEONE
INTO YOUR PAIN

You can't whitewash your sins and get by with it; you find
mercy by admitting and leaving them.

—PROVERBS 28:13 MSG

*S*in and pain love a good secret. You've got to be brave to tell that
shameful thing to those people you want to like you. But just try
it, and you'll be surprised. You'll be surprised how often people
give grace. You'll be surprised at how quickly the light eliminates the
darkness, and despite what your mind tells you, you will feel braver
once it's out in the open.

---

*Are you carrying shame over a certain sin or experience? Write about
it and plan to share it with someone.*

....

....

....

....

....

....

....

> *The darkness can't hang around when it's exposed in the light.*

....

....

....

....

....

....

....

....

....

....

....

....

Don't keep secrets. Tell somebody you trust. Please.

Day 65

>>>>> ————

DIVINE DETOURS

Many are the plans in a person's heart, but it is the LORD's purpose that prevails.

—PROVERBS 19:21 NIV

The Lord has given me divine detours more than once, where I've had to work through this question: *What if I don't actually get to do the thing I want to do?* Divine detours are no fun in the moment. Whether they involve work, dating, friendships, church, or family, they're a shock. They're a change in plans that you didn't ask for. But they take us where we're supposed to go in the long run.

What divine detour have you faced in the past? How did it end up taking you where you were supposed to go? What divine detour are you facing now?

....

....

....

....

....

....

....

A divine detour may just be God's way of getting you to look up at Him.

....

....

....

....

....

....

....

....

....

....

....

....

....

God sees the whole picture. You can trust Him,
even when He derails your plan.

Day 66

>>>>

WHY PERSEVERANCE MATTERS

Not only so, but we also glory in our sufferings, because we know that suffering produces perseverance; perseverance, character; and character, hope. And hope does not put us to shame, because God's love has been poured out into our hearts through the Holy Spirit, who has been given to us.

—ROMANS 5:3–5 NIV

I t comes way too easy for me to walk away from something that feels hard. But as I mature and grow up, I'm learning that courage builds when I persevere. Brave people realize that we rejoice in our sufferings because it leads to perseverance, and perseverance produces character, and ultimately, it brings us to the hope we have in Jesus. And hope is worth fighting for.

Is there something you're ready to walk away from? Do you think it would be better to persevere? Why or why not?

....

....

....

....

Hold on. Persevere.

....

....

....

....

....

....

....

....

....

....

....

....

Brave people don't give up.

Day 67

>>>> ————→

DON'T GIVE UP

Let us not become weary in doing good, for at the proper time
we will reap a harvest if we do not give up.

—GALATIANS 6:9 NIV

O kay, I'm going to tell you something, and I want you to listen.
Don't give up. Don't quit! You're on a journey. You're looking for
brave. You've been looking at your life—at your pain and joys
and calling—and you've been finding the brave. But don't quit now.
Looking for brave and doing things that are healthy for your mind,
body, and soul will reap a harvest of blessing.

—————————————————

*Now that you're more than halfway through this journal, how have you
seen bravery show up in your life, heart, or attitude since you began?*

....

....

....

....

....

....

....

....

*Don't quit trying
to find the brave in
your life.*

....

....

....

....

....

....

....

....

....

....

....

Looking for brave will reap a harvest of blessing.

Day 68

WHEN PAIN HEALS

On hearing this, Jesus said, "It is not the healthy who need a doctor, but the sick."

—Matthew 9:12 NIV

Our God is a healer. And there are times when God is going to take you through surgery, not because He wants to hurt you but because He loves you and wants to heal you. I've seen it in my own life—things being cut away, sins being revealed, secrets being exposed, all for my good. When we remember we're sinners in need of Jesus, we can trust our Great Physician.

When has God taken you through something painful in order to help you? How did your life change for the better? (It always does with God!)

....

....

....

....

....

....

....

....

....

....

> *We can be brave in the face of brokenness and pain and spiritual surgery because we know that God is good.*

....

....

....

....

....

....

....

....

....

....

Surgery hurts, but it is always for our good and for our health.

Day 69

GOD'S PURPOSE FOR YOUR BODY

Or do you not know that your body is a temple of the Holy Spirit within you, whom you have from God? You are not your own.

—1 CORINTHIANS 6:19 ESV

Jesus makes all things new. One day our bodies and this broken world will be totally healed. In the meantime, God has a purpose for your body—with all its imperfections and sicknesses. He wants to use you, as you are, to bring glory to Himself. Brave people look at the bodies they are in and choose to see them for what they are—vessels that hold a mighty God.

How do you feel about your body? How does it change the way you feel to realize your body is home to God's Spirit?

....

....

....

> *By God's grace, I've gone from thinking my body is never good enough to believing it's a temple of the Holy Spirit.*

Your health matters because only a working body can be a brave body.

>>>>————————>

RHYTHMS OF DISCIPLINE

For the moment all discipline seems painful rather than pleasant, but later it yields the peaceful fruit of righteousness to those who have been trained by it.

—Hebrews 12:11 esv

Your discipline, the rhythm that makes you the best you, shows up when it is time to say the right thing, do the right thing, be the brave person you want to be. What does it look like? I don't know for you. I just know that I often like to label discipline as something boring and unnecessary, when really discipline is the work done on the practice field so you are ready for the big game.

What are your rhythms of discipline, the things you do to train your body, mind, or spirit? What do you want to add to your routine?

....

....

....

....

....

....

If you want to be brave, you have to practice.

....

....

....

....

....

....

....

....

....

....

....

Practice makes perfect, and practice makes you brave.

Day 71

>>>>

PLEASE PLAY

This is the day that the LORD has made; let us rejoice and be glad in it.

—PSALM 118:24 ESV

It may not seem important or brave to make play a priority, but you have got to be brave to step away from responsibilities. To dismiss the lie that your career will fall apart if you spend some time having fun. Brave people know that it's not just okay to play. It's healthy. And if you don't make space in your life for play, you will burn out.

What do you like to do for fun? What can you do to break up your day with play?

....

....

....

....

....

> *Play is like a deep breath on a really hard journey of courage.*

....

....

....

....

....

....

....

....

....

....

....

....

....

....

....

You can have fun and laugh because God is in control.

Day 72

PLEASE EXERCISE

I appeal to you therefore, brothers, by the mercies of God, to present your bodies as a living sacrifice, holy and acceptable to God, which is your spiritual worship.

—ROMANS 12:1 ESV

Your size isn't the issue. A lifestyle of daily exercise is not about losing weight. It's about honoring your body and treating it well. Your body was meant to move; it was not meant to be still. You need your muscles and your bones to be strong enough to do all the things you were called to do for as many years as you're meant to be here.

What's your exercise routine? How can you make this time an act of play and of worship?

....

....

....

....

....

....

....

Just get out there and move your body.

....

....

....

....

....

....

....

....

....

....

....

....

Your body is a temple of God that you get to use for His glory.

Day 73

>>>> ─────

PLEASE EAT YOUR VEGGIES

So, whether you eat or drink, or whatever you do, do all to the glory of God.

—1 Corinthians 10:31 ESV

'm not saying you can never eat the burger. Burgers are fantastic, but if you thoughtlessly consume food that tastes good and fail to consume food that is actually good for you, you are not treating your body well. God has given your body to you for a reason. He has a purpose for your life. Be brave enough to make your eating habits intentional.

Think about your eating habits and your overall health. Can you make any dietary changes that will help you feel better from the inside out?

....

....

....

....

Moderation is key, friends.

....

....

....

....

....

....

....

....

....

....

....

....

Be thoughtful. Take care of this gift that is your body.

Day 74

>>>>

PLEASE REST

It's useless to rise early and go to bed late, and work your worried fingers to the bone. Don't you know he enjoys giving rest to those he loves?

—PSALM 127:2 MSG

Listen, I'm all about the hustle. You've got to work. You've got to say yes. You've got to try. But hustling for 365 days is not what brave people do. They stop when they need to stop, even if it's scary and a little bit costly. Your spiritual health is more important than that goal you're hustling toward. And you won't meet your goals if you burn out.

What are the benefits of rest? How can you make it a rhythmic part of your life?

....

....

....

....

....

....

....

....

> *Brave people recognize that there are times when you have to stop.*

....

....

....

....

....

....

....

....

....

....

....

....

Be brave enough to rest—knowing that you need it, that it's healthy.

Day 75

>>>> ———————→

SABBATH

"Do your work in six days and rest on the seventh day."

—Exodus 34:21 CEV

*B*rave friends, please choose to have a Sabbath. Unplug. Give yourself a break. Say yes to rest and yes to relationships. It takes courage to walk away from your job or your calling for a bit, believing that God will still provide. But Sabbath is something we are called to—a discipline that will make our lives better if we embrace it.

Describe what a day of rest and worship looks like to you. When can you take a Sabbath this week?

....

....

....

....

....

....

....

....

> *You've got to take time away from the grind. Regularly.*

....

....

....

....

....

....

....

....

....

....

We need Sabbath. We need rest.

Day 76

WORDS CAN HEAL

The words of the reckless pierce like swords, but the tongue of the wise brings healing.

—Proverbs 12:18 niv

Look at today's verse. Reckless words? They hurt. But words can heal too. Brave people don't gossip and use their words to hurt others. Brave people use their words to heal. Speaking with kindness about other people's hearts and minds *and* bodies can go a long way to heal. May you see the healing, feel the healing, that comes from the tongue of the wise.

What words spoken by others have been healing to you?

....

....

....

....

....

....

....

....

....

We have two options when we use our words: we can build or we can destroy.

....

....

....

....

....

....

....

....

....

....

Words. Are. Powerful. Use yours to build.

Day 77

>>>>————

HEALTHY PEOPLE THINK ABOUT OTHER PEOPLE

Jesus replied: "'Love the Lord your God with all your heart and with all your soul and with all your mind.' This is the first and greatest commandment. And the second is like it: 'Love your neighbor as yourself.' All the Law and the Prophets hang on these two commandments."

—Matthew 22:37–40 NIV

f you're truly being brave and if you're truly pursuing health, you grow to love yourself and you love other people out of that. To love someone is to believe in *them*. When someone believes in you, it changes everything—how you carry yourself, how you treat others, how you live day after day. You can give that same gift to those around you.

You have to love yourself before you can love others. Do you love yourself now? How can you grow to love yourself more?

....

....

....

> *You have to love yourself to love others well.*

....

....

....

....

....

....

....

....

....

....

....

Healthy, brave people love other people.

Day 78

BE A MENTOR

Follow my example, as I follow the example of Christ.

—1 Corinthians 11:1 NIV

The Bible challenges men and women to lead by example and also to teach and pour into those younger than they are, who are a few steps behind. A common roadblock for people is that they feel unqualified. Who am I to mentor someone? But if you're walking with Jesus, you have wisdom to pass down.

What wisdom can you pass down? Make a list of several lessons you've learned about life, relationships, God, callings, and so on, since beginning your walk with Jesus.

....

....

....

....

....

....

....

....

....

....

Brave people don't just pour into their own hopes and dreams. They pour their wisdom and time and love into others.

....

....

....

....

....

....

....

....

....

....

It is life-giving to take what the Lord's taught you and pass it down.

Day 79

>>> ———

BLAZE A TRAIL

Your word is a lamp to my feet and a light to my path.

—Psalm 119:105 esv

*Y*ou, my friend, married or single, female or male, you are blazing a trail with your life for the younger women and men behind you. You are making a way for them, saving them some pain that your bloodied arms prove is real and honoring their footsteps by providing a clear path. It never feels easy, and it never is free. But it is what we want more than anything else.

Who do you look to as a trailblazer—that is, someone who's had similar experiences as you and inspired or encouraged you? Who might look to you as a trailblazer?

....

....

....

....

....

....

....

> *We all need trailblazers.*

....

....

....

....

....

....

....

....

....

....

....

....

....

Never forget that you are a trailblazer.

Day 80

EVERYTHING YOU HAVE IS GOD'S

The earth and everything on it belong to the LORD. The world
and its people belong to him.

—PSALM 24:1 CEV

God gives us a new identity in Christ. Now we are His, and we
are stewards of His stuff. So your time, your money, all your
resources, even your story—it's God's, my friend. Living with
that understanding takes courage because we want to decide how to
live based on what we want. But everything you have is God's. So be
brave enough to steward everything you have in a way that displays
God's greatest generosity.

What does it look like to live like everything you have is God's?

....

....

....

....

....

....

....

*Living for self?
That's easy. Living
like everything
you have is God's
(because it is)?
That's brave.*

....

....

....

....

....

....

....

....

....

....

....

Are you brave enough to believe God has been generous to you?

Day 81

>>>>——————→

BE GENEROUS WITH
YOUR TIME

Share with the Lord's people who are in need. Practice hospitality.

—ROMANS 12:13 NIV

It's not easy to give your time to others. I get that. But serving other people, leading a small group, talking to your neighbor, whatever it is—that time is precious and that time is sacred, and God can love people supernaturally when you give them your time. Are you brave enough to be generous with your time, trusting that God has a purpose in it?

What changes do you want to make in how you spend your time?

....

....

....

....

....

....

....

....

God trusts us to be brave and to be generous with each day He gives us on the planet.

....

....

....

....

....

....

....

....

....

....

The time God has given us was created by Him and belongs to Him.

Day 82

BE GENEROUS WITH
YOUR WISDOM

*If any of you lacks wisdom, let him ask God, who gives
generously to all without reproach, and it will be given him.*

—JAMES 1:5 ESV

God is so generous with us. He gives good gifts to His children, and wisdom is such an incredible gift. So listen. This is where your bravery comes in. You've been given wisdom by God, liberally. (If you haven't, ask Him for it!) Brave people offer their wisdom liberally to others. (Not opinions. *Wisdom.*) Ask God to give you opportunities to share wisdom with others today.

*Be brave this week and find a way to share the wisdom He's given.
Maybe write a post on social media or send an encouraging note
to a friend.*

....

....

....

You are qualified to share godly wisdom because you have God.

....

....

....

....

....

....

....

....

....

....

....

He will give you wisdom, and you can give it to others.

Day 83

>>>>———————

BE GENEROUS WITH
YOUR MONEY

"No one can serve two masters, for either he will hate the one
and love the other, or he will be devoted to the one and despise
the other. You cannot serve God and money."

—MATTHEW 6:24 ESV

Jesus said you can't serve God and money. It just doesn't work. You
might think you don't love money more than God, but where is
your money going? Are you using your money in a way that honors Him? It's not easy. I know! But are you brave enough to believe that
if you are generous with your money, you won't run out?

*Think about your money habits. How much do you give to God? To
others? What changes do you want to make in how you spend your
money?*

....

....

....

....

....

God blesses us so richly when we are generous.

....

....

....

....

....

....

....

....

....

....

....

....

God uses our money to spread His love to others.

Day 84

>>>>———

BE GENEROUS WITH YOUR WORDS

Gracious words are like a honeycomb, sweetness to the soul and health to the body.

—Proverbs 16:24 esv

Have you ever been around someone whose words just grate? We can use our words to hurt others, to be negative, to gossip, and to complain. Or we can be brave enough to step out into a negative, cynical world, where people want to hear gossip and negativity, and instead we can be generous with our words and use them to bring life.

What does it mean to "bring life" with your words?

....

....

....

....

....

....

....

....

....

....

....

....

....

....

....

....

....

....

....

....

Be different in a world that uses words to hurt. Use your words to heal.

Be intentional and generous with your words
to yourself, to others, and to God.

Day 85

>>>>

BE GENEROUS WITH
YOUR HOME

Make sure you don't take things for granted and go slack in working for the common good; share what you have with others. God takes particular pleasure in acts of worship—a different kind of "sacrifice"—that take place in kitchen and workplace and on the streets.

—HEBREWS 13:16 MSG

For many, home is a sanctuary. It's a place you go to retreat from a world that can be so harsh and so dark. And being generous with your home isn't easy. You might just want to be by yourself. But brave people recognize that they can use their home to love others with the love of Christ. Brave people share—even their sanctuaries—with others.

Is opening your home hard or easy for you? Why?

....

....

> *Be brave enough to love the people around you.*

Brave people are generous with their homes.

WHAT YOU HAVE SHOULD AFFECT WHERE YOU ARE

Tell them to go after God, who piles on all the riches we could ever manage—to do good, to be rich in helping others, to be extravagantly generous. If they do that, they'll build a treasury that will last, gaining life that is truly life.

—1 Timothy 6:18–19 msg

Brave people deny themselves and serve others. Brave people are the ones who take what God's given them and give generously. Friend, your resources should make an impact. Be brave enough to put yourself, your wants, your money, and your time in second place, so that what you have—what God's given you to steward—makes a difference wherever you go.

How are you using what you have to make a difference in the world? How do you dream of making a bigger and bolder impact one day?

....

....

....

....

Your resources should be making a difference in this world—by furthering God's kingdom.

....

....

....

....

....

....

....

....

....

....

....

Show others the love of Christ in a tangible way.

Day 87

SACRED PLACES

"Do not come any closer," God said. "Take off your sandals, for the place where you are standing is holy ground."

—Exodus 3:5 NIV

Because we have this amazing access to the Father through Jesus, it's easy to get complacent and forget that our God is holy and deserves our awe. Yes, we can talk to Him wherever, but I think it's really important to have a sacred place with Him too. If you don't, it's hard to be intentional, and you've got to be intentional about your time with the Lord.

Where is your sacred space, the place where you intentionally seek time with Him? If you don't have one, what place in your home or community could you try out?

....

....

....

....

....

....

....

You can't expect to be brave without spending time with God.

....

....

....

....

....

....

....

....

....

....

....

....

Your sacred space doesn't have to be fancy.
Just find a spot and make it sacred.

Day 88

>>>>———————

BE PRESENT WHERE
YOU ARE

"My command is this: Love each other as I have loved you."

—JOHN 15:12 NIV

Wherever you live, wherever you work, wherever you hang out, be all there. For me to do that, I have to put my phone down sometimes. Maybe you're not a big phone person. Maybe it's TV for you or a good book. You know the thing you turn to when you want to escape. But loving others means being present with them in their pain and their joy. It means being all there.

———————————

Can you identify the things that distract you, things you turn to when you want to escape?

....

....

....

....

....

....

....

....

Are you brave enough to believe that you're not missing out on something else?

....

....

....

....

....

....

....

....

....

....

Be intentional about being present where you are.

Day 89

>>>>

WHERE YOU MEET
WITH GOD

Let the heavens rejoice, let the earth be glad; let the sea resound,
and all that is in it. Let the fields be jubilant, and everything in
them; let all the trees of the forest sing for joy.

—PSALM 96:11–12 NIV

Spending time in God's creation, in His presence, will make you
brave. You can be brave because you're God's. Today, even if it's
just stepping outside of your office building and sitting under a
tree, spend time in creation and remember how loved you are and how
brave you can be.

Where will you go to spend time in God's creation today?

....

....

....

....

....

....

....

....

His love makes me brave, and there is no place I love to meet with God more than sitting in His creation.

....

....

....

....

....

....

....

....

....

....

....

Just sit. Just be. Sometimes the Lord just wants to hang out.

Day 90

>>>>

YOUR HOME

My friends, you were chosen to be free. So don't use your freedom as an excuse to do anything you want. Use it as an opportunity to serve each other with love.

—GALATIANS 5:13 CEV

How can you be brave in your home with the people you live with? Will you invite someone to stay with you for a while? Are you brave enough to be kind to your spouse? Can you unload the dishwasher first? In the places where you find the most comfort, you have to have a little extra something to give there. I think it's brave.

What does it look like to serve and be brave in your home?

....

....

....

....

....

....

....

....

....

Home is where we find peace, so to sacrifice in that place is to sacrifice deeply.

....

....

....

....

....

....

....

....

....

....

Courage often looks like sacrifice and service.

Day 91

>>>>> ————

YOUR NEIGHBORHOOD

"The second is this: 'Love your neighbor as yourself.' There is no commandment greater than these."

—MARK 12:31 NIV

*J*esus said the second greatest commandment was to love your neighbors. We can absolutely take this verse to mean all other people, but, friend, you've got actual neighbors all around you who need to know that hope is found in Jesus. Do you know them? How are you serving them and caring about them? Be brave enough to see the people around you and serve them.

How well do you know the people who live around you? What are some ways you can get to know them better?

....

....

....

....

....

How is your neighborhood different because you live in it?

....
....
....
....
....
....
....
....
....
....
....
....
....
....
....

Be brave enough to love the people around you. God will use you, friend.

Day 92

>>>> ————

YOUR CITY

"Also, seek the peace and prosperity of the city to which I have carried you into exile. Pray to the LORD for it, because if it prospers, you too will prosper."

—JEREMIAH 29:7 NIV

When you think about the puzzle of the person you are, the zip code on your mailing address is an important piece. So what does it look like to love the city you're in? Even if you wish you lived somewhere else right now, even if you're here just for a season, God has placed you in your city for a purpose. Be brave in your city.

How are you being brave—serving and loving others—in the city where you live now?

....

....

....

....

....

....

....

....

> *It takes courage to serve in new places just down the street.*

....

....

....

....

....

....

....

....

....

....

....

....

Being brave at home means serving.

Day 93

>>>>

YOUR COUNTRY

Let every person be subject to the governing authorities. For there is no authority except from God, and those that exist have been instituted by God.

—ROMANS 13:1 ESV

No matter what your country's government looks like right now, you can be brave in it. Being brave looks like praying for your leaders to come to Christ. It looks like loving the people in your country and sticking to your biblical values. It looks like respecting your country even if you don't agree with everything your country's leadership is doing.

What do you like about your country? What changes would you like to see made?

....

....

....

....

....

....

....

> *No matter what the political state of things may be, you can be brave.*

....

....

....

....

....

....

....

....

....

....

....

....

Brave people trust God with who is or isn't in authority over them.

Day 94

>>>———

THE WORLD

And [Jesus] said to them, "Go into all the world and proclaim
the gospel to the whole creation."

—MARK 16:15 ESV

I f you've never had a moment when no one around you speaks your
language or shares your pigment or knows how elementary school
works, you need to go. You need to see that the world is big and
diverse, and maybe God doesn't look or sound the way you always
thought He did, because the world has a lot of different-looking and
different-sounding people, all of whom are made in His image. Do
whatever it takes to expand your map.

*Is there a place outside of your country you'd like to visit? Where and
why? How can you be brave there?*

....

....

....

....

If you go where you've never gone before, you will see God like you've never seen Him before.

You need to see how other places and people view God.

Day 95

>>>> ———————→

JERUSALEM

Pray for the peace of Jerusalem: "May those who love you be secure. May there be peace within your walls and security within your citadels."

—Psalm 122:6–7 NIV

We've talked about the power of prayer, and y'all, it is real. Prayer changes things. So when you pray for places like your home and your neighborhood and your city and your country and the world, pray for Jerusalem—the *only* city God specifically asks us to pray for. Pray for the bravery of those who are being persecuted for their beliefs. Pray for a revival. Pray.

Begin praying for Jerusalem today. Pray for its people and prosperity.

....

....

....

....

....

....

....

We are asked by God to pray for the peace of Jerusalem.

....

....

....

....

....

....

....

....

....

....

....

....

....

....

Prayer is our most direct connection to God—your voice to His ear.

Day 96

JESUS WAS BRAVE

"If the world hates you, keep in mind that it hated me first."

—JOHN 15:18 NIV

I t stokes my fire of courage, remembering that Jesus did some majorly brave things right here—right where I am. Single like me. Human like me. Tempted like me. And He took a risk on me. He asked His disciples to do the same. To give up everything to follow Him. To live bravely, as He did—pouring out His life for a hurting, hostile world. And He asks us to do the very same thing.

What are some of your favorite brave things Jesus did on earth?

....

....

....

....

....

....

> *The world hated Jesus, but He was brave enough to give His life for it anyway.*

The Son of God came to do the most courageous thing this planet has ever seen.

Day 97

JESUS IS BRAVE

> Then I saw heaven opened, and behold, a white horse! The one
> sitting on it is called Faithful and True.
>
> —Revelation 19:11 esv

John 3:16 says it all. God is holy and we are sinners. But Jesus bridged that gap; His death and resurrection cleared that path. And one day Jesus is coming back, not as the baby in the humble manger, but as the mighty King of kings and Lord of lords.

He deeply loves you and deeply knows you and is doing the hard work of forgiving again and again. Jesus is brave, and He made you to be brave too.

How does bravery help you carry on Jesus' work?

....

....

....

....

....

....

....

....

Jesus is still alive and still working for our good today.

....

....

....

....

....

....

....

....

....

....

....

....

Jesus wasn't just brave in the past tense. Jesus is brave today.

Day 98

>>>>———

YOU WERE MADE
TO BE BRAVE

Then David said to Solomon his son, "Be strong and courageous and do it. Do not be afraid and do not be dismayed, for the LORD God, even my God, is with you. He will not leave you or forsake you, until all the work for the service of the house of the LORD is finished."

—1 CHRONICLES 28:20 ESV

Courage isn't just for mighty warriors. It's for you. It's for your relationship with God. It's for your dreams and your calling and your work. It's for your relationships with fellow humans. You can be brave during all the changes of life. You can be brave in the face of pain. You can be brave with your health. Brave with your money. Brave wherever you are!

When you look back at the time you've spent in this journal and in God's Word, how do you see your life touched and improved by courage?

....

....

....

....

> There is not an area of your life that can't be touched and improved by courage.

....

....

....

....

....

....

....

....

....

Your God will not leave you. And because you know that, you are brave.

Day 99

>>>>————→

YOU ARE BRAVE

Take a good look at God's wonders—they'll take your breath away.

—Psalm 66:5 MSG

When you started this one-hundred-day journey, I bet you were challenging yourself, taking brave steps, and all the while feeling terrified. But flip through these pages and look at how brave you are. Take this day to reflect on the awesome miracles God has performed for you and in you and in the people around you. Your brave choices have ripple effects. Brave people inspire those around them to be brave.

Flip back through your journal. What has God done in you and through you to show that you are brave?

....

....

....

....

....

....

....

Do you see now that you are braver than you know?

....

....

....

....

....

....

....

....

....

....

....

All glory for any bravery we exhibit goes straight to Jesus.

Day 100

>>> ———————→

LET'S ALL BE BRAVE

"The LORD your God is with you, the Mighty Warrior who saves. He will take great delight in you; in his love he will no longer rebuke you, but will rejoice over you with singing."

—ZEPHANIAH 3:17 NIV

Making brave choices in your life is going to change the world. At the least, it will change *your* world. But I dare not limit what you are going to do on this planet, friend. Your life is Jesus' reward for His suffering—your brave yeses, your courageous nos, all of it. Today I pray courage for you—the deep, deep kind that changes the way you live. Now hold your map and the hand of your Father. And let's all be brave.

―――――――――――――――――――――――――――――――――――

How have your brave choices already changed your world? What brave thing will you do next?

....

....

....

> *It's so important for you to be brave.*

People are waiting and God is watching to see
where your courage will take you.

YOU ARE
brave!